The Cotswolds was created by man and nature working in close harmony. Nature supplied the raw materials - oolitic limestone, crossed by sparkling clear springs. Man supplied the ingenuity, muscle and craftsmanship - genius that transformed the stone into humble cottages and stately mansions, soaring churches or simple burial mounds.

The Cotswolds has been declared an area of outstanding natural beauty.

There is, however, some doubt over the origins of the name. Some believe an Anglo-Saxon called Cod owned a lot of wolds in the Windrush area (wold means upland common). This led to 'Cod's Wold'. Others believe the name derives from 'cote' meaning a sheepfold.

Evidence of man's early work on the landscape can be found in the prehistoric relics such as Hetty Pegler's Tump, Belas Knap and Notgrove. These are stone-built earth-covered burial mounds, some 4,500 years old. As part of his worship ritual, Bronze Age man arranged the stones in circles or henges.

The Romans arrived in AD 43 and criss-crossed the Cotswolds with their roads - the Fosse Way, Akeman Street and Ermine Way. They also developed Cirencester into the second most important town in the land. It is now regarded as the 'capital of the Cotswolds'.

The wealth of the Cotswolds came from wool. By the 14th to 16th centuries, the area was prosperous. Sheep graziers, wool merchants and clothiers amassed great fortunes from the trade in wool and cloth. From such fortunes were built the great 'wool churches' of Cirencester, Chipping Campden, Northleach, Fairford and Wotton-under-Edge. Local craftsmen created masterpieces in stone.

After Henry VIII swept away the power and assets of the church in the 16th century, the shift of fortune in favour of lords of the manor led to the building of graceful Cotswold manor houses.

The area's history is everywhere represented in stone. In fact, it is said that a native Cotsaller can do anything with the stone except eat it.

The limestone comes in many varieties and shades, from golden in Bath, silvery in Painswick, honey coloured in Chipping Campden and tawny brown to the north of the region. When freshly dug from the ground, it is easy to work, which is why the carving to be seen in churches, market crosses and houses is exquisitely fine. On exposure to the air, the stone hardens and endures centuries of weathering. Some beds of stone are in thin layers and on exposure to the frost, they split. These are graded into different sizes and used for roof tiles.

In the 18th and 19th centuries, the stone was used to create dry-stone walling to enclose the land. But by then, the commercial success of the wold-and-wool combination had started to decline. The textile trade became more mechanised and moved to a new centre in the industrial north. As a consequence, the Cotswold's cosy cottage industry suffered the bitter hardship of a severe recession.

Yet because it escaped the desecration of zealous massive modernisation and re development, the Cotswolds has retained its timeless, traditional charm for the visitor today. The allure of the area is such that three Cotswolds houses have been chosen by members of the royal family as their chosen country homes: The Prince of Wales at Doughton near Tetbury, the Princess Royal at Gatcombe Park near Minchinhampton and Prince and Princess Michael of Kent at Nether Lypiatt near Stroud.

This illustrated guide highlights the Cotswolds' finest features.

Die Cotswolds genannte Gegend Englands entstand durch enge, harmonische Zusammenarbeit von Mensch und Natur. Natur lieferte das Rohmaterial - oolithischen Kalkstein, durchzogen von klaren Quellen. Der Mensch lieferte den Einfallsreichtum, die Arbeitskraft und das handwerkliche Geschick, mit denen der Stein zu bescheidenen Häusern und herrschaftlichen Anwesen, prunkvollen Kirchen und einfachen Grabstätten verarbeitet wurde.

Die Geschichte dieser Gegend ist überall in Stein zu finden. Es heißt, daß ein einheimischer "Cotsaller" alles mit dem Stein machen kann, nur nicht essen.

Der Kalkstein kommt in vielen Sorten und Farbtönen, in Bath ist er goldgelb, in Painswick silbrig, in Chipping Camden honigfarben und im Norden der Gegend gelbbraun. Frisch aus dem Boden gehauen läßt er sich leicht bearbeiten, was die feinen Steinskulpturen und -ornamente in Kirchen, an Marktkreuzen und Häusern erklärt. An der Luft wird der Stein hart und kann den Witterungseinflüssen jahrhundertelang standhalten. Einige der Gesteinsschichten bestehen aus dünnen Steinlagen, die sich spalten, wenn sie Frost ausgesetzt sind. Diese Steine werden nach Größen sortiert und für Dachziegel verwendet.

Die als Cotswolds bezeichnete Gegend wurde offiziell zu einem Gebiet besonderer Naturschönheit erklärt. Niemand weiß jedoch genau, wo seine Grenzen zu ziehen sind.

Der landschaftliche Reiz dieser Gegend ist so beeindruckend, daß sich drei Mitglieder des englischen Königshauses Cotswold-Häuser als offiziellen Landwohnsitz gewählt haben: Doughton bei Tetbury gehört dem Prinzen von Wales, Gatcombe Park bei Minchinhampton ist Prinzessin Annes Wohnsitz und Nether Lypiatt bei Stroud gehört dem Prinzen und der Prinzessin von Kent.

Dieser illustrierte Reiseführer hebt die schönsten Orte und Sehenswürdigkeiten der Cotswolds hervor.

La région des Cotswolds a été créée par l'homme et la nature oeuvrant en synergie. La nature a fourni les matières premières - un paysage de calcaire oolithique regorgeant de sources d'eau gazeuse cristallines. L'homme y a apporté son ingéniosité, sa force, et le génie de l'exécution qui ont transformé la pierre en cottages modestes et en manoirs majestueux, en églises aux flèches élancées et en tumulus tout simples.

L'histoire de cette région est omniprésente dans la pierre. En fait, on dit qu'une personne originaire des Cotswolds peut tout faire avec de la pierre, excepté la manger.

Le calcaire existe dans différentes variétés et divers tons; du calcaire au ton doré de Bath à celui au ton argenté de Painswick, en passant par la teinte miel de Chipping Campden et le brun fauve typique du nord de la région. Lorsqu'on vient de l'extraire, il est facile à travailler et c'est la raison pour laquelle les sculptures que l'on peut voir dans les églises, les croix de marchés et les maisons, sont si belles et délicates. Exposé à l'air, le calcaire durcit et peut résister aux intempéries pendant des siècles. Certaines couches rocheuses sont fines et se fendent lorsqu'il gèle. Elles sont classées en fonction de leur tailles et utilisées pour les tuiles de toiture.

La région connue sous le nom de Cotswolds a été officiellement déclarée comme une région de toute beauté. Mais personne n'est sûr de son étendue.

Elle présente un tel attrait que trois maisons des Cotswolds ont été choisies par des membres de la famille royale pour leur maison de campagne. Le Prince de Galles à Doughton, près de Tetbury, la Princesse Royale à Gatcombe Park près de Minchinhampton et le Prince et la Princesse Michael de Kent à Nether Lypiatt, près de Stroud.

Ce guide illustré vous fera découvrir les merveilles des Cotswolds.

BURFORD

Burford's prosperity was built on wool and cloth. Trading took place in the wide main street, lined with fine old houses, which dips down to the River Windrush. Across the river is a stone medieval bridge.

Burford's nearby quarries provided the stone not just for the domestic needs of the local people, but was chosen to build architectural masterpieces such as Blenheim Palace and many of Oxford's colleges - notably the Sheldonian Theatre. Burford's master masons were much in demand after the Great Fire of London in the 17th century to help Sir Christopher Wren rebuild St Paul's Cathedral and the City churches.

Straddling the major main coaching routes in this part of the country, Burford's inns became famous. King Charles II and his mistress Nell Gwynn stopped at the George Hotel when visiting nearby Bibury Races.

The almshouses and the church largely date from the 15th century. The church was much restored in the 1870s by a zestful vicar who resisted critics of the scheme (who included artist William Morris) with the defiant declaration: "The church Sir is mine, and if I choose to I shall stand on my head in it." The Tolsey (Market Hall) is now a museum.

Burfords Wohlstand beruhte auf Wolle und Tuch. Austragungsort für den Handel war die breite Hauptstraße mit schönen alten Häusern, die zum Windrush hinunterführt. Über den Fluß führt eine mittelalterliche Steinbrücke.

Die Steinbrüche in der Nähe von Burford lieferten nicht nur den Stein für den Bedarf der Einheimischen, sondern auch das Material zum Bau architektonischer Meisterstücke, wie Blenheim Palace und vielen der Colleges in Oxford.

Burford doit sa prospérité à sa laine et à ses étoffes. Ce commerce avait lieu dans la rue principale, très large et bordée de vieilles maisons magnifiques, qui descend vers la Windrush. Un pont médiéval en pierres enjambe la rivière.

Les carrières à proximité de Burford ont d'une part apporté les pierres nécessaires pour les habitants locaux, et d'autre part ont été choisies pour construire des chefs-d'oeuvre d'architecture tels que Blenheim Palace et de nombreux collèges d'Oxford.

CHELTENHAM

Pigeons pecking at salt crystals from a mineral spring triggered the expansion of Cheltenham from a humble market town to a fashionable and elegant Regency spa town. The first pump room was built in the 18th century by retired sea captain Henry Skillicorne and the mineral waters were claimed to be effective for "bilious conditions, obstruction of liver, spleen and perspiration". King George III came for a five-week stay to take the "medicinal" waters of Cheltenham. When the national hero, the Duke of Wellington, was later relieved of a liver disorder, Cheltenham's success was firmly established, though not everyone was convinced of the water's curative powers: William Cobbett described the town's people as "East India plunderers, West Indian floggers, English tax-gorgers, together with gluttons, drunkards and debauchees of all descriptions". They were, he alleged, in Cheltenham to get rid of "the bodily consequences of their manifold sins and iniquities."

The town - complete with racecourse - was built around the spa for the socialite seekers of good health. It now boasts some of the finest Regency buildings and squares in Britain.

Notable among them is Montpellier Street, built by architect John Papworth, which features shops embellished by caryatids, or female figures. The Rotunda, with spectacular marbled interior, once dispensed water but now (as a bank) cash. The Royal Crescent echoes, but does not quite rival, the architectural splendours of Bath. At the end of the Promenade is the Pittville Pump Room, a Regency mansion which copies a classical Athens temple. Cheltenham mineral water can still be sampled here, as can a display which depicts the development of Cheltenham through fashion.

Die Stadt, komplett mit Pferderennbahn, wurde um den Kurort für die erholungsbedürftigen und gesundheitsbewußten Angehörigen der feinen Gesellschaft herum aufgebaut. Heute kann sie einige der besten Gebäude und Plätze der Regency-Epoche in Großbritannien vorzeigen.

Eine sehenswerte Straße ist die Montepellier Street, die vom Architekten John Papworth gebaut wurde und mit Karyatiden, weiblichen Statuen, verzierte Ladenfronten hat. An der Rotunde mit ihrer spektakulären Marmorausstattung erhielt man früher Kurwasser, heute ist sie eine Bank. Die Gebäudereihe des Royal Crescent ahmt die architektonische Pracht von Bath nach, kann ihr aber nicht

La ville - et son hippodrome - a été construite autour des thermes pour les membres de la haute société qui se préoccupaient de leur santé. Elle possède maintenant certains des plus beaux édifices et des plus belles places Régence du pays.

L'une des plus remarquables est Montpellier Street, construite par l'architecte John Papworth, qui regorge de magasins ornés de cariatides ou statues de femmes. Jadis on se rendait à La Rotonde, avec son intérieur extraordinaire en marbre, pour aller chercher de l'eau, on va maintenant y chercher des espèces. Le Royal Crescent évoque, sans y être totalement comparable, l'architecture splendide de Bath. Au bout de la Promenade, se trouve la "Pump Room" de Pittville, un manoir Régence qui est la copie d'un temple classique d'Athènes. On peut toujours goûter l'eau minérale de Cheltenham et on peut y admirer une exposition qui dépeint les développements de Cheltenham par le biais de la mode.

vollständig gleichkommen. Am Ende der Promenade liegt der Pittville Pump Room, die Trinkhalle, eine nach dem Vorbild eines klassischen Tempels von Athen erbaute Regency-Villa. Man kann hier immer noch Cheltenham-Mineralwasser probieren. Sehenswert ist auch ein Display, auf dem die modebedingte Entwicklung von Cheltenham dargestellt wird.

CHIPPING CAMPDEN

Chipping Campden has a quiet, laid back charm. At its heart is the 17th century Market Hall which gives a clue to the place itself: Chipping means market and for two centuries wool was traded within this arcaded centrepiece in the High Street. The wide High Street is made up of the buildings of prosperous merchants, dating from the 14th century. Notable buildings include the Woolstaplers Hall, Dover's House and the Regency Cotswold House Hotel. The lofty 15th century church contains memorials to noted wool tycoons, including one to William Grevel, described as "The Flower of the wool merchants of all England". Another benefactor of Chipping Campden was Sir Baptist Hicks, first Viscount Campden, who built the Market Hall and the almshouses and a mansion which (except for the restored gateway) was burnt down during the Civil War.

Nearby Dovers Hill, owned by the National Trust, was the site of the Cotswold Olympick Games for two centuries. Started in 1612 by attorney Robert Dover after a friend at court obtained the King's permission, they consisted mainly of sporting feats of skill, speed and strength. But they included Cotswold shin-kicking competitions. Contestants used to train for the event by having their shins beaten by a plank or a hammer. Other crowd pullers were cock-fighting, coursing and dancing for virgins. The Olympicks were banned in 1851 by the rector who deplored the rowdy antics of the gangs who were attracted by the games. The Olympicks have been revived (held on the evening of the first Friday following Spring Bank Holiday) though the 20th century version is much tamer than the original.

Chipping Campden strahlt einen ruhigen, zwanglosen Reiz aus. In der Ortsmitte liegt die Market Hall aus dem 17. Jahrhundert, die auf den Ursprung des Ortsnamens hinweist: "Chipping" bedeutet Markt. Zwei Jahrhunderte lang war dieses Arkadengebäude in der High Street ein Austragungsort des Wollhandels. Die breite High Street setzt sich aus den Gebäuden wohlhabender Kaufleute aus dem 14. Jahrhundert zusammen.

Die hohe Kirche aus dem 15. Jahrhundert enthält Gedenktafeln an bedeutende Wollmagnate, darunter eine an William Grevel, der als "Die Blume der Wollhändler ganz Englands" beschrieben wird. Ein weiterer Gönner von Chipping Campden war Sir Baptist Hicks, der erste Viscount Campden, der die Market Hall, die Armenhäuser und ein Herrenhaus baute, das (mit Ausnahme des restaurierten Tors) während des Bürgerkriegs niedergebrannt wurde.

Chipping Campden possède un charme tranquille et paisible. La Halle du 17ème siècle, située au coeur de ce village, donne une idée de cet endroit; Chipping signifie "marché" et pendant deux siècles on a fait le commerce de la laine dans cet édifice central orné d'arcades dans la Grande Rue. La Grande Rue est composée de bâtiments qui appartenaient aux marchands prospères et datent du 14ème siècle. L'église élancée du 15ème siècle contient des monuments à la mémoire des grands magnats de la laine, dont un à la mémoire de William Grevel, décrit comme "La Fleur des marchands de laine dans toute l'Angleterre". Un autre bienfaiteur de Chipping Campden était Sir Baptist Hicks, premier Vicomte Campden, qui a fait construire la Halle, les hospices et un manoir qui (à l'exception de son portail restauré) a été brûlé pendant la Guerre Civile.

CHIPPING NORTON

'Ceapen' (which slurred into Chipping) is an old English word meaning market and a market has been flourishing here since the 13th century. Wool was traded in large quantities and the town grew fat on the proceeds. The 'wool' church of St Mary features fine stone tracery windows dating from the 14th and 15th centuries. Nearby stands a 17th century group of almshouses.

Topping and tailing the market place are the classical-style Town Hall and the Old Guildhall. While fine 18th century buildings grace the wide main streets, Chipping Norton's back lanes are clustered with tiny cottages where cloth weavers used to work.

The town is the highest in Oxfordshire. North of Chipping Norton are the Rollright Stones, a 100 ft prehistoric stone circle arranged between 1500-2000 BC as a focus for worship and burial. The stones are popularly known as the King's Men, a reference to the legendary army turned into stone by a local witch. One solitary stone is said to represent the king and five standing stones his Whispering Knights.

"Ceapen" (aus dem später "Chipping" wurde) ist ein altes englisches Wort, das Markt bedeutet. In Chipping Norton blüht schon seit dem 13. Jahrhundert ein Markt. Der Ort ist die höchste Stadt in der Grafschaft Oxfordshire. Nördlich von Chipping Norton befinden sich die Rollright Stones, ein 35m hoch prähistorischer Steinkreis, der zwischen 1500 und 2000 vor Christi Geburt für Andachts-und Bestattungszwecke verwendet wurde.

"Ceapen" (qui par la suite donna "Chipping") est un vieux mot anglais qui signifie "marché", et le marché est une activité prospère de cette ville depuis le 13ème siècle. Cette ville est la plus élevée dans l'Oxfordshire. Le nord de Chipping Norton est constitué par les Rollright Stones, un cercle de pierres préhistoriques de 35 m, érigé aux alentours de 1500-2000 avant J.-C. comme un lieu de culte et de sépulture.

GLOUCESTER

The Romans established a fort at the gateway to Wales - the lowest crossing of the River Severn - and Glevum grew up to be one of their most important centres in Britain. Remains of the Roman influence can still be seen today in the City Wall and the layout of the main streets which meet at the Cross. Mosaics, sculptures and artifacts from the period are carefully preserved in Gloucester's Museum.

Old Glevum became Gleawcester in Anglo Saxon times. When the country was divided into shires it became the capital of its own shire. Following the 11th century Norman Conquest, William the Conqueror took the decision at Gloucester to start the Domesday survey of his captured kingdom. Shortly after, in 1089, work started on the great new abbey church of St Peter, the basis of Gloucester's greatest glory.

The chapter house, the oldest surviving part of the cathedral, is one of the nation's architectural treasures. The nave with its great pillars was completed in

1124 and the spectacular Early English vaulting a century later. The great 14th century east window contains the coloured glass heraldic arms of those who fought in the Battle of Crecy and Siege of Calais in 1346 and 1347. The pinnacled tower, built a century later, soars to 225 feet. The cathedral's two most famous monuments are the tomb of King Edward II who was murdered at Berkeley Castle in the 14th century and the wooden effigy of Robert, Duke of Normandy, son of William the Conqueror. The fan vaulting in the cloisters is considered to be the finest in Britain.

Other places of interest include the half-timbered Bishop Hooper's Lodgings, now a folk museum; Gloucester Docks and the Tailor of Gloucester's house, a Beatrix Potter Museum.

Am Tor zu Wales - dem niedrigsten Überquerungspunkt des Flusses Severn - bauten die Römer ein Fort, Glevum, das sich zu einem ihrer wichtigsten Zentren in Großbritannien entwickelte. Der römische Einfluß zeigt sich noch heute in der Stadtmauer und der Anordnung der Hauptstraßen der Stadt, die am "Cross" (Kreuz) zusammenlaufen.

Der Kapitelsaal, der älteste noch vorhandene Teil der Kathedrale, ist einer der architektonischen Schätze des Landes. Das Hauptschiff mit seinen großen Säulen wurde im Jahr 1124 fertiggestellt, das imposante frühenglische Gewölbe ein Jahrhundert später. Das Buntglas des großen Ostfensters aus dem 14. Jahrhundert enthält die Wappen derer, die in der Schlacht von Crecy 1346 und der Belagerung von Calais im Jahr 1347 kämpften. Der ein Jahrhundert später gebaute spitze Kirchturm ist ca. 70 m hoch. Das Fächergewölbe in den Kreuzgängen gilt als das beste in Großbritannien.

Les Romains établirent jadis un fort à la limite du Pays de Galles - le point le plus bas du fleuve Severn - et Glevum devint alors l'un des centres romains les plus importants de Grande-Bretagne. On peut encore admirer les vestiges de l'influence romaine aujourd'hui; la Muraille de la Ville et l'agencement des rues principales, qui convergent vers la Croix.

La salle capitulaire, qui est la plus vieille partie de la cathédrale ayant survécu, est l'un des trésors architecturaux du pays. La nef avec ces grands piliers a été terminée en 1124 et la voûte spectaculaire "Early English" un siècle plus tard.

La magnifique fenêtre Est du 14ème siècle contient les armoiries de ceux qui ont participé à la Bataille de Crécy et au Siège de Calais en 1346 et 1347. La tour et son clocheton, construite un siècle plus tard fait 70 m de haut. La voûte en éventail du cloître est considérée comme la plus belle de Grande-Bretagne.

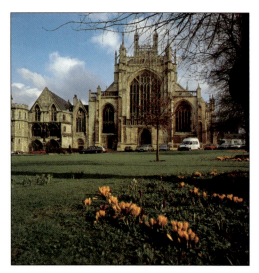

HIDCOTE MANOR

Sandwiched between the quaintly named Hidcote Boyce and Hidcote Bartrim is Hidcote Manor, dating from 1663. Its garden has been described as "one of the most delightful in England". Now owned and tended by the National Trust and open to the public, the garden was created this century by Major Lawrence Johnston. It consists of a series of small gardens of different mood and character which display interesting and rare plant species. The individual gardens are separated by walls and hedges, giving the whole a feeling of a "house open to the sky".

Das zwischen den beiden Orten Hidcote Boyce und Hidcote Bartrim liegende Herrenhaus Hidcote Manor wurde 1663 erbaut. Sein Park wurde als "einer der bezauberndsten in England" beschrieben. Hidcote Manor befindet sich heute im Besitz des National Trust und ist der Öffentlichkeit zugänglich. Der Park wurde in diesem Jahrhundert von Major Lawrence Johnston geschaffen.

Situé entre les sites aux noms pittoresques Hidcote Boyce et Hidcote Bartrim se trouve Hidcote Manor, qui remonte à 1663. Son jardin a été décrit comme "l'un des plus beaux d'Angleterre". Ce jardin qui appartient au National Trust, chargé de son entretien, est ouvert au public et a été créé durant ce siècle par Major Lawrence Johnston.

MORETON-IN-MARSH

The Fosse Way is the road built by the Romans across the Cotswolds to link Cirencester with Bath. Moreton-in-Marsh grew up where the Fosse crossed the Worcester Road and its main trade in the 13th century was catering for travellers.

It is now a pleasant market town studded with picturesque old houses and inns along an exceptionally wide main street.

The Roman road lying beneath the modern tarmac was often flooded, which some believe is the reason behind Moreton-in-Marsh's name. Others declare it derives from the fact that it refers to the 'march' or boundary of four counties which is marked nearby.

Moreton-in-Marsh has strong links with Oxford University. Its oldest building is the 16th century Curfew Tower which tolled the curfew until 1860.

King Charles I slept at the White Hart Royal Hotel for one night in 1644 -
"When friends were few and dangers near
King Charles found rest and safety here."

Market Hall, just over a century old, was donated by Lord Redesdale to the local council in 1951.

Fosse Way ist die von den Römern durch die Cotswolds gebaute Straße, die Cirencester mit Bath verbindet. Moreton-in-Marsh entstand, wo der Fosse Way die Worcester Road überkreuzte. Im 13. Jahrhundert war der Ort in erster Linie auf die Unterbringung und Verpflegung von Reisenden ausgelegt.

Heute ist Moreton-in-Marsh ein hübsches Städtchen mit vielen malerischen alten Häusern und Gaststätten entlang einer außergewöhnlich breiten Hauptstraße.

La Fosse Way est une route construite par les Romains, qui traverse les Cotswolds pour relier Cirencester à Bath. Moreton-in-Marsh s'est développée à l'emplacement où la Fosse croisait la Route de Worcester, et son commerce principal au 13ème siècle était la restauration pour les voyageurs de passage.

C'est aujourd'hui une ville de marché agréable parsemée de vielles demeures et d'auberges pittoresques le long d'une rue principale exceptionnellement longue.

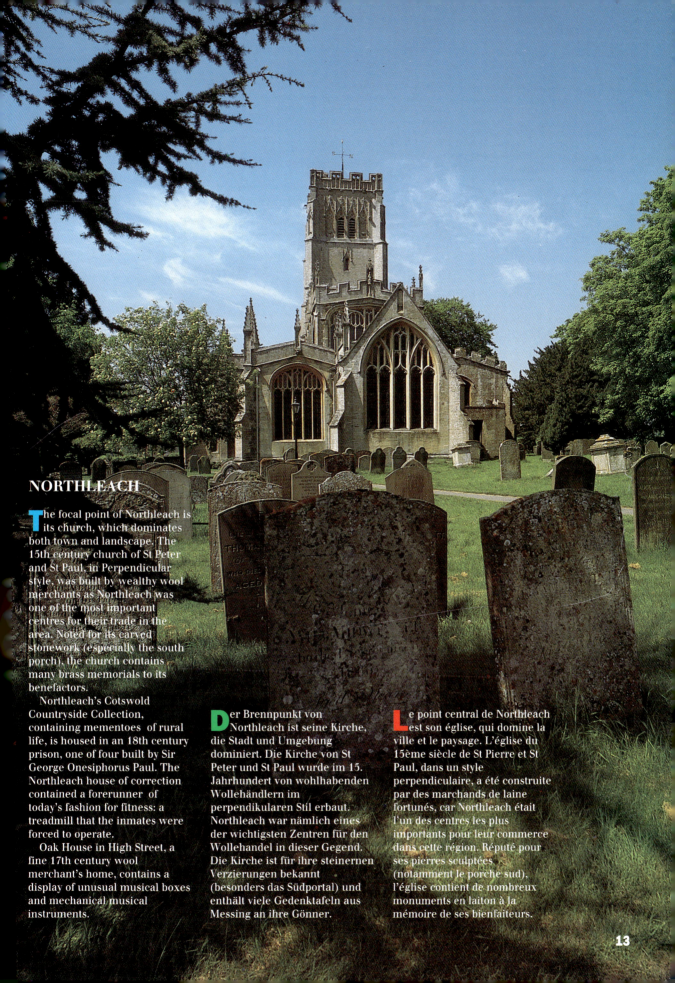

NORTHLEACH

The focal point of Northleach is its church, which dominates both town and landscape. The 15th century church of St Peter and St Paul, in Perpendicular style, was built by wealthy wool merchants as Northleach was one of the most important centres for their trade in the area. Noted for its carved stonework (especially the south porch), the church contains many brass memorials to its benefactors.

Northleach's Cotswold Countryside Collection, containing mementoes of rural life, is housed in an 18th century prison, one of four built by Sir George Onesiphorus Paul. The Northleach house of correction contained a forerunner of today's fashion for fitness: a treadmill that the inmates were forced to operate.

Oak House in High Street, a fine 17th century wool merchant's home, contains a display of unusual musical boxes and mechanical musical instruments.

Der Brennpunkt von Northleach ist seine Kirche, die Stadt und Umgebung dominiert. Die Kirche von St Peter und St Paul wurde im 15. Jahrhundert von wohlhabenden Wollehändlern im perpendikularen Stil erbaut. Northleach war nämlich eines der wichtigsten Zentren für den Wollehandel in dieser Gegend. Die Kirche ist für ihre steinernen Verzierungen bekannt (besonders das Südportal) und enthält viele Gedenktafeln aus Messing an ihre Gönner.

Le point central de Northleach est son église, qui domine la ville et le paysage. L'église du 15ème siècle de St Pierre et St Paul, dans un style perpendiculaire, a été construite par des marchands de laine fortunés, car Northleach était l'un des centres les plus importants pour leur commerce dans cette région. Réputé pour ses pierres sculptées (notamment le porche sud), l'église contient de nombreux monuments en laiton à la mémoire de ses bienfaiteurs.

UPPER AND LOWER SLAUGHTER

Though less than half a mile apart, the two villages are linked by the River Eye around which golden stone Cotswold cottages gather. Stone footbridges provide the crossing over the clear water from one lawned bank to the other.

There is some doubt whether the villages are named from the Anglo-Saxon word 'slohtre' (muddy place) or from 'slah treow', a reference to the many sloe trees in the area. Then again, the medieval lords of the manor were the 'de Solotres'.

Lower Slaughter has a red-brick 19th century corn mill.

The Tudor Upper Slaughter Manor, considered one of the finest in the Cotswolds, is now a hotel. It was built on the site of a 15th century priory. The church has Norman roots and was built on the site of a castle whose mound remains in the centre of the village.

Die beiden Dörfer liegen zwar kaum einen Kilometer voneinander entfernt, sind aber durch den Fluß Eye verbunden, um den sich kleine Cottages aus goldgelbem Cotswolds-Stein sammeln. Fußgänger können das klare Gewässer über steinerne Brücken zwischen grasbewachsenen Ufern überqueren.

Bien que ces deux villages soient à moins d'un kilomètre l'un de l'autre, ils sont reliés par la rivière Eye entourée de cottages des Cotswolds en pierres aux tons doré. Les passerelles en pierre permettent d'enjamber les eaux claires pour passer d'une rive verdoyante à l'autre.

SNOWSHILL

Snowshill crowns a hill overlooking the Vale of Evesham. The village Manor was once owned by Kenulf, King of Mercia, who gave it to the Abbey of Winchcombe in 821. The Manor house seen today (owned by the National Trust) dates from around 1500, although the front was remodelled in 1700. Another King, Henry VIII, gave Snowshill Manor to his wife Catherine Parr after the Dissolution of the monasteries. Charles Paget Wade, whose fortune was based on sugar, bought the Manor early this century and not only restored the house and gardens, but packed into it his collection of craftsmanship - boneshaker bicycles, musical instruments, clocks, toys, weavers' and spinners' tools, nautical objects and banners. His family arms, Nequid pereat, mean 'let nothing perish'.

In contrast, the village cottages form a humble but harmonious stone fringe on the hillside.

Snowshill liegt auf einem Hügel und überblickt das Vale of Evesham.

Das Herrenhaus (im Besitz des National Trust) stammt etwa aus dem Jahr 1500, seine Front wurde jedoch 1700 umgebaut. Im Gegensatz dazu bilden die Dorfhäuser einen bescheidenen aber harmonischen steinernen Saum an der Seite des Hügels.

Snowshill surplombe une colline qui domine le Vale of Evesham.

Le manoir (qui appartient au National Trust) remonte à 1500, bien que sa façade ait été remodelée en 1700.

Par contraste, les cottages du village forment une bordure en pierre modeste, mais harmonieuse sur le versant de la colline.

STANTON

Stanton can be regarded as a stone version of the Sleeping Beauty story. Since the 16th and 17th centuries, its looks have barely altered with the passing of time. The careful preservation of Stanton owes much to architect Sir Philip Scott who bought the estate in which the village lies at the beginning of this century and ensured the restoration was undertaken with sensitivity and care. The restored church with Norman origins contains traces of 14th century wall paintings and some 15th century glass. The high street, which features a medieval village cross, climbs towards Shenberrow Hill, site of an Iron Age camp.

Stanton kann als eine steinerne Version des Dornröschen-Märchens betrachtet werden. Der Ort scheint sich seit dem 16. und 17. Jahrhundert kaum verändert zu haben.

Die Hauptstraße mit ihrem mittelalterlichen Dorfkreuz zieht sich zum Shenberrow Hill hinauf, auf dem sich eine Eisenzeit-Niederlassung befand.

Stanton peut être considérée comme une version en pierre d'un décor de la Belle au Bois-Dormant. Depuis les 16ème et 17ème siècles, son apparence n'a pratiquement pas changé.

La grande rue, qui comporte une croix de village médiévale, monte vers Shenberrow Hill, site d'un camp de l'Age de Fer.

STANWAY

Stanway's name - 'stane or stone way' - gives a clue to the mellow golden glories of this famous Cotswold village. The yellow Guiting stone is mined nearby and the village is a worthy advertisement for the local quarry.

Stanway House, now owned by the Earl of Wemyss and March, features an impressive Jacobean gatehouse. The house, one of the finest manor houses of that age in the Cotswolds, stands on land formerly owned by Tewkesbury Abbey.

The tithe barn of Stanway, now the social focal point for the village, dates from 1400. The church, with medieval origins, has been greatly restored to a point that purists now tend to dismiss its features. But as part of the scene which takes in the manor gatehouse in a tree-studded setting, it is one of the most photographed sites in the area.

Stanways Name, "Steinweg", ist ein Stichwort für den warmen goldengelben Stolz dieses berühmten Cotswolds-Dorfes. Der gelbe Guiting-Stein wird hier in der Nähe gebrochen, und das Dorf ist ein hervorragendes Aushängeschild für den örtlichen Steinbruch.

Stanway House, das sich im Besitz des Grafen von Wemyss und March befindet, verfügt über ein imposantes Pförtnerhaus aus der Zeit Jakobs I. Stanway House ist eines der prächtigsten Herrenhäuser aus dieser Zeit in den Cotswolds. Das Land, auf dem es erbaut ist, gehörte früher zum Kloster Tewkesbury.

Le simple nom "Stanway" - "voie de pierre" - donne une idée des merveilles aux tons dorées et doux que l'on peut admirer dans ce célèbre village des Cotswolds. La pierre jaune de Guiting est extraite non loin de là et le village est la meilleure publicité, à juste titre, pour sa carrière locale.

Stanway House, qui appartient maintenant au Comte de Wemyss and March, possède une loge jacobine impressionnante. Le manoir, l'un des plus beaux des Cotswolds qui datent de cette époque, se dresse sur les terres qui appartenaient jadis à l'Abbaye de Tewkesbury.

STOW-ON-THE-WOLD

Several roads meet at Stow-on-the-Wold. At its heart is the unspoilt large central space with the old market place: Stow quickly became a thriving market town (as many as 20,000 sheep changed hands on one occasion) and the traditional market cross survives. Stow's horse fair in May is still a major event, although its greatest trade today is antiques, crafts and works of art in the shops around the market square.

Stow's St Edward's church features a 14th century tower. A church has occupied the site for more than a thousand years. During the 17th century, the church was used to imprison hundreds of Royalists after the Civil War's last stand at the Battle of Stow.

The hilltop town's exposed position led to the local rhyme "Stow-on-the-Wold where the wind blows cold". It is the highest point crossed by the Roman Fosse road.

In Stow-on-the-Wold laufen mehrere Straßen zusammen. Seinen Kern bildet die noch ursprüngliche Ortsmitte mit dem alten Marktplatz. Stow wurde schnell zu einem blühenden Marktstädtchen (bis zu 20.000 Schafe wechselten hier an einem Tag den Besitzer), dessen traditionelles Marktkreuz heute noch steht. Der Pferdemarkt von Stow im Mai ist zwar immer noch eine größere Veranstaltung, den größten Handelszweig bilden heute jedoch die Läden am Marktplatz, die hauptsächlich Antiquitäten, Handwerksartikel und Kunstgegenstände anbieten.

Plusieurs routes se croisent à Stow-on-the-Wold. Au cœur de ce village encore intact se trouve la grande place centrale avec la vieille place du marché; Stow est rapidement devenue une ville de marché prospère (20.000 moutons ont été vendus en une seule fois, à cet endroit par le passé) et la croix traditionnelle du marché a survécu. La foire aux chevaux, qui a lieu en mai, est toujours un événement capital. On trouve également des antiquités, pièces d'artisanat et des oeuvres d'art dans les magasins qui entourent la place du marché.

SUDELEY CASTLE

Sudeley has been fortified by a castle for nine centuries. Its historic zenith was in the 16th century when it passed from royal hands to Sir Thomas Seymour, brother of Queen Jane, third wife of King Henry VIII. After the king died, his sixth wife Katherine Parr married Sir Thomas and came to Sudeley Castle. Her tomb lies in Sudeley Church, in the castle grounds.

Both castle and church were damaged during the Civil War. The castle was used as the Royalists' military base, led by Prince Rupert. After a fierce siege, it was taken by the Parliamentarians and wrecked. The 19th century was a time of restoration for both church and castle: Sir Gilbert Scott, architect, restored the church in the 1860s and the Dent family restored and rebuilt the castle interiors and laid out the formal gardens.

Sudeley ist schon seit neun Jahrzehnten mit einer Burg befestigt. Seinen historischen Höhepunkt hatte es im 16. Jahrhundert, als es aus königlichem Besitz an Sir Thomas Seymour überging, den Bruder von Jane Seymour, der dritten Gemahlin von Heinrich VIII. Nach dem Tod des Königs heiratete seine sechste Gemahlin, Katherine Parr, Sir Thomas und zog nach Sudeley Castle. Ihr Grab befindet sich auf dem Gelände von Sudeley Castle.

Sudeley a été fortifié par un château pendant neuf siècles. Son apogée historique eut lieu au 16ème siècle lorsqu'il passa des mains des monarques aux mains de Sir Thomas Seymour, le frère de la reine Jane, troisième femme du Roi Henri VIII. Après la mort du roi, sa sixième femme, Katherine Parr, a épousé Sir Thomas et est venue vivre à Sudeley Castle. Elle repose dans l'église de Sudeley, sur les terres du château.

TEWKESBURY

Tewkesbury grew up at a point where the rivers Severn and Avon meet. The fine Norman tower of the Abbey church of St Mary dominates the skyline.

At Tewkesbury, the dominance of stone gives way to half-timbered houses and inns. The town is studded with courts, cul-de-sacs and alleys and boasts the area's oldest inn, the Black Bear.

Tewkesbury entstand an einem Punkt, an dem die Flüsse Severn und Avon aufeinandertreffen. Der eindrucksvolle normannische Turm der Klosterkirche von St Mary dominiert die Silhouette der Stadt.

In Tewkesbury finden sich mehr Fachwerkgebäude als die sonst vorherrschend aus Cotswold-Stein gebauten Häuser.

La ville de Tewkesbury s'est développée au point de jonction du fleuve Severn et de l'Avon et la splendide tour romane de l'église St Mary de l'Abbaye domine toujours le ciel de cette ville.

A Tewkesbury, la prédominance de la pierre fait place aux maisons et auberges à colombage.

WINCHCOMBE

In Saxon times, Winchcombe was capital of the shire of Winchcombshire in the kingdom of Mercia. King Ceonwulf founded a monastery in the eighth century and shortly after, or so the story goes, the Pope in Rome received an account via a 'dove from heaven' of the murder of Kenelm, his righful heir. Other supernatural signs led to Kenelm's martyrdom. His tomb in the abbey then became a shrine visited by pilgrims from far and wide.

The abbey itself became rich and powerful over the centuries until it was bought by Lord Seymour of Sudeley at the 16th century Dissolution of the Monasteries. Lord Seymour pulled the old abbey down, but two stone coffins, said to be those of Kenelm and his father, are preserved in the nave of Winchcombe's church, St Peter's. The church is ringed with a fascinating series of carved grotesques and gargoyles and among its treasures inside is an altar cloth embroidered by Katharine of Aragon.

Vineyard Street, lined with small cottages and pollarded limes, probably took its name from the vines which grew in this sheltered part of the town. Certainly Tobacco Close takes its name from the cultivation of tobacco to which enterprising locals switched when the wool trade started to go into decline.

In Vineyard Street's old ducking pond, scolding wives and witches were ducked in the water. The town is also famous for its medieval galleried inn, the George - used by pilgrims to the abbey - and the quaintly named Old Corner Cupboard Inn.

Winchcombe ist bekannt für seine "Vineyard Street", dt. Weingarten-Straße, die mit kleinen Cottages und gekappten Linden umsäumt ist und ihren Namen wahrscheinlich von den Reben erhielt, die in diesem geschützten Teil der Stadt wuchsen. Tobacco Close wurde auf jeden Fall nach dem Anbau von Tabak genannt, auf den geschäftstüchtige Einwohner umstellten, als es mit dem Wollehandel bergab ging.

Im alten Dorfteich in Vineyard Street wurden früher böse Weiber und Hexen durch Untertauchen bestraft. Die Stadt ist auch für ihr mittelalterliches Gasthaus mit Gallerie, den George Inn, in dem das Kloster besuchende Pilger übernachteten, und den Old Corner Cupboard Inn mit seinem schnurrigen Namen berühmt.

Vineyard Street, à Winchcombe, bordée de petits cottages et d'arbres écimés, doit probablement son nom aux vignes qui poussent dans cette partie abritée de la ville. Tobacco Close doit sans aucun doute son nom à la culture de tabac qui a pris la suite du commerce de la laine lorsque ce dernier connut son déclin.

Jadis, on punissait les épouses acariâtres et les sorcières de la ville en les plongeant dans l'eau de la mare de Vineyard Street. Cette ville est également célèbre pour son auberge à galeries médiévale, "The George" - utilisée par les pèlerins qui se rendaient à l'abbaye - et pour l'auberge qui porte le nom pittoresque "Old Corner Cupboard Inn".

SOUTH COTSWOLDS

BADMINTON HOUSE

Yes, this was where the game with the shuttlecock originated. Badminton is now synonymous with another sport, the International Horse Trials held in the park each spring. It is also the centre of the Beaufort Hunt, with whom some members of the present royal family enjoy riding.

The Dukes of Beaufort have made the Palladian style Badminton House their home for over three centuries. It was built by the first Duke in the 17th century then enlarged by the third Duke. The house contains a fine collection of paintings and furniture and stands in a 15,000 acre parkland setting.

Das im palladianischen Stil erbaute Badminton House ist schon seit über drei Jahrhunderten der Sitz der Herzöge von Beaufort. Das Landhaus enthält eine feine Gemälde- und Möbelsammlung und liegt in 6000 ha Parklandschaft.

Les Ducs de Beaufort ont fait de Badminton House, au style palladien, leur demeure depuis plus de trois siècles. Elle renferme une magnifique collection de tableaux et de meubles et se dresse dans un parc de 6000 hectares.

BIBURY AND ARLINGTON

Bibury hugs one side of the River Coln; Arlington the other. While Bibury swaggers under the description of Victorian artist, William Morris, as "the most beautiful village in the Cotswolds", Arlington's famous row of 17th century stone cottages is probably the most photographed scene in the entire area.

Bibury's church dates back to Saxon times, with a Norman porch. Bibury Court, a hotel, has a 17th century wing said to have been designed by Inigo Jones.

Arlington Mill Museum and Gallery displays the working machinery of the old corn mill, together with collections of implements and furniture that formed part of rural Cotswold life.

Rack Isle is a water meadow once used for drying cloth on racks after it had been worked by the weavers in the cottages in Arlington Row. Both are owned by the National Trust.

Bibury liegt an einem Ufer des Flusses Coln, Arlington am anderen. Während Bibury stolz auf die Beschreibung des viktorianischen Künstlers William Morris als "das schönste Dorf in den Cotswolds" verweist, ist Arlingtons berühmte Reihe von Cottages aus dem 17. Jahrhundert wahrscheinlich die am meisten fotografierte Szene der ganzen Gegend.

Bibury se blottit sur l'une des rives de la rivière Coln, Arlington sur l'autre. Bien que Bibury puisse se vanter d'être, conformément à la description de l'artiste William Morris, de l'ère victorienne, "le plus beau village des Cotswolds", la célèbre rangée de cottages en pierres du 17ème siècle d'Arlington est probablement la scène la plus photographiée de toute la région.

BISLEY

In a fold of the hills high in the Toadsmoor valley, Bisley beckons those who enjoy tall tales and charming traditions. The hill has been revered for some thousands of years. Certainly the Romans worshipped the seven springs which gush down the hillside. Now known as Bisley Wells, the Seven Springs are blessed and decorated with flowers on Ascension Day - a ceremony known as "well dressing". The custom dates from 1863, started by the village vicar, Thomas Keble, whose brother John was an important figure in the Church of England.

Over Court is associated with the Bisley Boy legend. When she was 10, Princess Elizabeth (later Queen Elizabeth I) was reputed to have 'died' while staying there. Her hosts were so afraid of telling her father, King Henry VIII, the bad news that they supposedly buried the body secretly and substituted a red-haired boy in her place. This theory explains why the queen, in later years, went bald and remained a virgin.

The fantastic story started over a century ago when a stone coffin was unearthed in Bisley churchyard. For many years before its burial the coffin - containing the remains of a girl - was in the grounds of Over Court.

Bisley churchyard contains a unique 13th century well head incorporating the Poor Soul's Light, used to hold candles for prayers for those parishioners too poor to buy their own.

Bisley also has a double lock up, designed in 1824 to cool down local sinners.

In einer Bodenfalte in den Hügeln tief im Toadsmoore Valley lockt Bisley die Liebhaber von Märchen und bezaubernden Traditionen. Schon die Römer verehrten die sieben Quellen, die hier entspringen. Bisley Wells, wie die Sieben Quellen jetzt heißen, werden jedes Jahr an Christi Himmelfahrt in einer "Well Dressing" genannten Zeremonie mit Blumen geschmückt und geweiht.

Niché dans l'une des collines, dominant la vallée de Toadsmoor, Bisley enchante tous ceux qui adorent les histoires et les traditions pleines de charme. Jadis, les Romains rendaient un culte aux sept sources qui jaillissent sur ce versant, et de nos jours ces Sept Sources, qui sont connues sous le nom de Bisley Wells (puits de Bisley), sont bénies et décorées de fleurs, le jour de l'Ascension - une cérémonie connue sous le nom de "well dressing" (décoration des puits).

CASTLE COMBE

Castle Combe is a picture-book Cotswold village. Set deep in a valley, it takes its name from the remains of a Norman castle on the hilltop above. In medieval times, Castle Combe was a celebrated sheep and wool centre with a charter to hold a fair. The Market Cross stands at the village centre. The Dower House and Manor House (now a hotel) are both 17th century. The heavily restored church contains a fine tomb effigy of one of the early lords of the manor, Walter de Dunstanville. He is depicted in full chain mail armour.

Castle Combe ist ein malerisches Cotswolds-Bilderbuch-Dorf. Das tief in einem Tal gelegene Dorf ist nach den Resten einer normannischen Burg auf dem Hügel über dem Ort benannt. Im Mittelalter war Castle Combe ein gefeiertes Zentrum für den Schaf- und Wollehandel und hatte einen Freibrief zur Durchführung eines Jahrmarkts. Das Marktkreuz steht in der Ortsmitte.

Castle Combe est un village des Cotswolds qui sort tout droit d'un livre d'images. Encastré dans une vallée, il doit son nom aux vestiges d'un château normand qui dominait la colline. Au Moyen Age, Castle Combe était un centre réputé pour ses moutons et sa laine et détenait une charte pour y organiser une foire. La croix de la place du marché se trouve au centre du village.

CIRENCESTER

Cirencester's heyday was some two thousand years ago, when, as Corinium Dobunnorum, it was the largest town outside London. The Roman settlers politely named their new development after local tribes, the Dobunni. Poised at the meeting point of three main routes, the Roman town became an important administrative centre with fine temples, a forum and a basilica. The Roman legacy today includes traces of the town wall in the abbey grounds and the turfed amphitheatre which was used for public entertainments. The town's Corinium Museum treasures include floor mosaics and the five-line word square puzzle which conceals the Christian invocation, Pater Noster:
ROTAS
OPERA
TENET
AREPO
SATOR

The Saxons plundered and burnt Corinium in the sixth century and renamed it Coryn Ceastre or Cirencester. It was known that King Canute held a great council meeting here in the 11th century. With the coming of the Normans, a great abbey was founded.

The wool trade rebuilt the town's fortunes in medieval times. Cirencester's great church of St John the Baptist has a wealth of carving and features an elaborate porch with notable fan vaulting. The chancel east window is filled with 15th century glass and the tower, which dates from that century, rises to 162 feet.

Cirencester's backstreets contain their own delights - almshouses, weavers' cottages, the remains of the Hospital and Chantry of St John the Evangelist. Cirencester Park has been in the family of the Earls Bathurst for three centuries. While the park is open to the public, the 18th century mansion in the grounds is private.

Cirencester hatte seine Blütezeit vor etwa zweitausend Jahren, als sie - Corinium Dobunnorum genannt - nach London die größte Stadt des Landes war.

Das römische Erbe der Stadt findet sich heute in Überresten der Stadtmauer auf dem Gelände der Abtei und im grasbewachsenen Amphitheater, das für öffentliche Unterhaltungsveranstaltungen verwendet wurde.

Cirencesters große Kirche "St John the Baptist" (Johannes der Täufer) ist reich an Schnitzereien und verfügt über ein kunstvolles Portal mit beachtenswertem Fächergewölbe. Das Buntglas im Ostfenster des Chors ist aus dem 15. Jahrhundert, und der ebenfalls im 15. Jahrhunderte erbaute Kirchturm ist ca. 50 m hoch.

Die Seitensträßchen von Cirencester haben ihren eigenen Reiz, hier findet man Armenhäuser, Weberhäuschen sowie die Reste eines Hospitals und der Kapelle des Heiligen Johannes des Predigers. Cirencester Park ist schon seit drei Jahrhunderten im Besitz der Earls Bathurst Familie.

Cirencester a atteint son apogée, il y a quelque deux mille ans, lorsqu'elle s'appelait "Corinium Dobunnorum", et était la plus grande ville après Londres.

L'ère romaine a laissé des vestiges tels que la muraille de la ville sur le terrain de l'abbaye et l'amphithéâtre recouvert de gazon qui était utilisé, jadis, pour les divertissements publics.

La magnifique église Saint Jean-Baptiste de Cirencester regorge de sculptures et possède un porche très orné avec une splendide voûte en éventail. La fenêtre Est du choeur présente des vitraux du 15ème siècle et la tour, également du 15ème siècle, fait 50 m de haut.

Les petites rues de Cirencester sont également de toute beauté - avec leurs hospices, cottages de tisserands, les vestiges de l'Hospital and Chantry de Saint Jean l'Evangéliste. Le parc de Cirencester appartient à la famille des Comtes Bathurst depuis trois siècles.

THE DUNTISBOURNES

Duntisbourne Abbots, Duntisbourne Leer and Duntisbourne Rouse are united by the Dunt stream. Duntisbourne Abbots was once church land owned by the abbots of Gloucester. Its church dates back to Norman times. Duntisbourne Leer was once owned by the abbey of Lire in Normandy. A ford crosses the Dunt here. The church at Duntisbourne Rouse is built on a steep dip down to the Dunt. The building has Saxon origins, but is largely Norman. Medieval wall paintings still survive.

Die Dörfer Duntisbourne Abbots, Duntisbourne Leer und Duntisbourne Rouse sind durch den Fluß Dunt verbunden.

Duntisbourne Abbots, Duntisbourne Leer et Duntisbourne Rouse sont unis par le cours d'eau Dunt.

EASTLEACH TURVILLE AND EASTLEACH MARTIN

These two small villages are separated by the river Leach but joined by a stone bridge known as Keble's bridge. The Kebles were lords of the manor of Turville in the 16th and 17th centuries. Unusually, the two village churches face each other across the Leach. Eastleach Martin's church was founded by one of William the Conqueror's knights and some of its original Norman features remain. Eastleach Turville's church has a Norman doorway and a 14th century saddleback tower.

Diese beiden kleinen Dörfer sind durch den Fluß Leach getrennt, aber über eine als "Keble's Bridge" bekannte Steinbrücke verbunden. Im 16. und 17. Jahrhundert waren die Kebles die Herren des Guts Turville. Die Dorfkirchen der beiden Dörfer sind sich über den Fluß hinweg zugewandt, was recht ungewöhnlich ist.

Ces deux petits villages sont séparés par la rivière Leach mais reliés par un pont en pierres connu sous le nom de pont de Keble. Les Kebles étaient les châtelains de Turville aux 16ème et 17ème siècles. Et fait inhabituel, les églises de ces deux villages se font face, séparées par la Leach.

FAIRFORD

Fairford's church was built by one of the Cotswolds' greatest wool merchant families, the Tames. The church is famous for its stained glass windows, 28 in all, the only complete set of late medieval glass of its type in the country. The windows are a vivid 'visual aid', telling the story that forms the basis of the Christian faith. They are regarded as unique examples of late fifteenth century art. The church also features a series of carvings beneath the choir stalls.

The church's massive central tower, which bears the arms of John Tame, has four stone 'guardians' or grotesques at each corner. A modern stone memorial by the porch celebrates the life of Tiddles the church cat, 1963-80.

The church overlooks the water meadows of the River Coln.

The noted cleric and poet John Keble was born in Fairford, in Keble House in London Road, in 1792. Keble College, Oxford, was founded in his memory.

At the local airfield, Concorde was tested. Nearby, Cotswold Water Park spreads over some hundred flooded gravel pits with facilities for fishing, sailing, waterskiing and birdwatching.

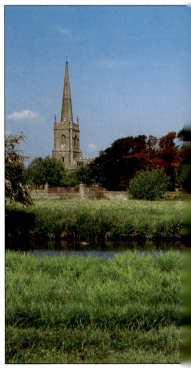

Die Kirche von Fairford wurde von einer der größten Wollehändlerfamilien der Cotswolds, den Tames, gebaut. Sie ist berühmt für ihre Buntglasfenster, insgesamt 28, die den einzigen kompletten Satz von spätmittelalterlichem Glas dieser Art in England darstellen.

Auf dem örtlichen Flugplatz wurde die Concorde getestet. Der Cotswolds Water Park in der Nähe von Fairford erstreckt sich über etwa hundert Baggerseen (ehemalige Kiesgruben), an denen man angeln, segeln, Wasserski fahren und Vögel beobachten kann.

L'église de Fairford a été construite par l'une des plus grandes familles de marchands de laine des Cotswolds, les Tames. L'église est célèbre pour ses vitraux, 28 au total, le seul ensemble complet de vitraux médiévaux de ce type dans le pays.

Le Concorde a été testé sur le terrain d'aviation de cette ville. A proximité se trouve le Parc Aquatique Cotswold qui comprend des centaines de carrières de graviers renfermant des plans d'eau pour la pêche, la voile, le ski nautique et l'observation des oiseaux.

LECHLADE

Lechlade is where the rivers Coln and Leach join the Thames and Inglesham. Not surprisingly, watery pursuits feature highly in the town's attractions. St John's bridge dates from the 13th century; Ha'penny Bridge from the 18th. In summer time, many boats moor on the river banks between the two bridges. The church, a fine example of Perpendicular architecture, has a slender spire, carved vestry door and noted chancel roof with carved bosses. The tranquil setting of the churchyard inspired the poet Shelley to compose his Summer Evening Meditation.

Lechlade liegt dort, wo die Flüsse Coln und Leach in die Themse münden und auf Inglesham treffen. Es überrascht deshalb nicht, daß viele von Lechlades Sehenswürdigkeiten am und im Wasser zu finden sind. Die Brücke St John's Bridge stammt aus dem 13. Jahrhundert, die Ha'penny Bridge aus dem 18. Jahrhundert. Im Sommer legen viele Boote an den Flußufern zwischen den beiden Brücken an.

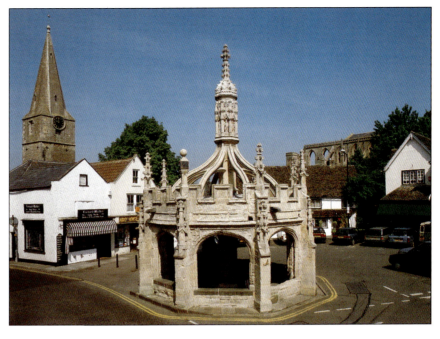

Lechlade se situe à la jonction des rivières Coln et Leach, de la Tamise et d'Inglesham. Il n'est donc pas surprenant que les activités nautiques soient les attractions principales de la ville. Le pont St John remonte au 13ème siècle et le pont Ha'penny au 18ème siècle. En été, de nombreux bateaux mouillent sur les rives entre ces deux ponts.

MALMESBURY

Malmesbury claims to be the oldest borough in England, receiving its royal charter in the year 924, though it was a thriving centre centuries before that. It was also one of the most important centres for pilgrims since the earliest stirrings of Christianity in Britain. A monastery was established here in 640 and a magnificent Benedictine Abbey was later built by the Normans on the site. Though most of it has collapsed, the remaining richly carved south porch is awesome in size and grandeur. Malmesbury Abbey Church contains the early 14th century monument of King Athelstan.

Market Cross dates from the 15th century when Malmesbury was a weaving centre. The beautiful Cross is over 40 feet high and richly carved. St John's Bridge crosses the River Avon. Nearby are 17th century almshouses on the site of the 13th century hospital of St John of Jerusalem, of which just a blocked doorway still stands.

Malmesbury gilt als die älteste Stadtgemeinde Englands und erhielt ihren königlichen Freibrief im Jahr 924. Sie war jedoch schon Jahrhunderte vorher ein blühendes Zentrum. Seit den frühesten Anfängen der Christenheit in Großbritannien war Malmesbury auch ein wichtiger Wallfahrtsort. Im Jahr 640 wurde hier ein Kloster gegründet, auf dessen Gelände die Normannen später eine prächtige benediktinische Abtei bauten. Diese Abtei ist heute zwar weitgehend zerfallen, aber das verbleibende, reich mit Steinornamenten verzierte Südportal ist in seiner Größe und Erhabenheit immer noch ehrfurchtgebietend. In der Klosterkirche von Malmesbury befindet sich das Grabmal des König Athelstan aus dem frühen 14. Jahrhundert.

Das "Market Cross" stammt aus dem 15. Jahrhundert, als Malmesbury ein Zentrum des Weberhandwerks war. Das Kreuz ist über 12 m hoch und reich verziert.

Malmesbury se vante d'être la plus vieille municipalité d'Angleterre; elle a reçu sa charte royale en l'an 924, mais était un centre commercial prospère depuis de nombreux siècles déjà. C'était également l'un des centres les plus importants de pèlerinage depuis les tout débuts du christianisme en Grande-Bretagne. Un monastère a été construit dans cette ville en l'an 640 et une magnifique Abbaye Bénédictine a été construite plus tard par les Normands à cet endroit. Bien qu'il n'y ait plus que quelques vestiges de cette abbaye, on peut encore admirer le porche sud, richement sculpté et magnifique de par sa taille et sa majesté. L'Eglise de l'Abbaye de Malmesbury contient le monument du roi Athelstan, qui remonte au début du 14ème siècle.

La Croix du Marché date du 15ème siècle, époque à laquelle Malmesbury était un centre de tissage. La Croix magnifique fait plus de 12 m de haut et est richement sculptée.

NAILSWORTH

Built at the junction of two deep valleys, Nailsworth's side streets are so steep that one is even called Nailsworth's Ladder. The town is regarded as 'nouveau' by Cotswolds connoisseurs: most of its main buildings are less than two centuries old. At its centre is the clock tower and war memorial, built in 1951. Reminders of its past as a clothmaking town can be seen in the old mills, notably Egypt Mill, now restored and transformed into a restaurant.

Nailsworth liegt am Kreuzungspunkt zweier tiefer Täler. Die Seitensträßchen des Orts sind sehr steil, eines sogar so sehr, daß man es "Nailsworth's Ladder", d.h. Nailsworths Leiter, nannte.

Ce village a été construit à la jonction de deux vallées profondes et ses rues latérales sont si pentues que l'une d'elle s'appelle "Nailsworth Ladder" (Echelle de Nailsworth).

OAKSEY WOODS

Oaksey Woods, near Kemble, is a colourful spring wonderland thickly carpeted with bluebells.

Owned by Lord Oaksey, whose father Lord Justice Lawrence took part in the Nuremburg trials, the privately-owned woods are nevertheless shared with the public.

The natural peace of the woods was touched by tragedy in January 1943 when a Halifax bomber flying from nearby Kemble airfield crashed. Foxgloves now cover the area of the recently unearthed wreckage.

Im Frühling ist Oaksey Woods in der Nähe von Kemble ein blaues Wunderland mit einem dichten Teppich blühender Sternhyazinthen.

Au printemps, Oaksey Woods, près de Kemble, est une merveille de couleurs recouverte d'un tapis de jacinthes des bois.

OWLPEN MANOR

Owlpen is one of the quietest corners of the Cotswolds. Its air of timeless tranquility is its special delight. In a deep hollow enclosed by woodlands, Owlpen has been a settlement since Saxon times. Today it largely comprises a manor house which dates from the 15th century, a Court House, a small Victorian church and a tiny 18th century mill.

Owlpen ist eine der ruhigsten Ecken der Cotswolds. Es besteht im wesentlichen aus einem Herrenhaus aus dem 15. Jahrhundert, einem Gerichtsgebäude, einer kleinen viktorianischen Kirche und einer winzigen Mühle aus dem 18. Jahrhundert.

Owlpen est l'un des coins les plus tranquilles des Cotswolds. Il comprend principalement un manoir qui date du 15ème siècle, un palais de justice, une petite église victorienne et un tout petit moulin du 18ème siècle.

PAINSWICK

Painswick's story is based on ewes and yews. The wool trade (with its associated dyed-cloth offshoot) brought prosperity to the small market town in the 17th and 18th centuries. But it is the churchyard yews of St Mary's that bring the visitors today. There are said to be 99 clipped yew trees, mostly planted in the late 18th century. By legend, only 99 will grow at any one time as the Devil kills the hundredth. The trees are clipped in September and a ceremony has evolved around it. Churchgoers encircle the church and hold hands to sing a Clipping Hymn. Children taking part wear flowers in their hair and each receive a token, a Painswick bun and a coin. The churchyard also features a series of table tombs in which the cloth merchants were buried. The 19th century stocks in nearby St Mary's Street punished "those who carry on carousels to the annoyance of neighbours".

The silver grey tones of the stone are seen to best advantage in the nearby houses and mansions - the Court House, Castle Hale and the half timbered Post Office and Little Fleece.

Half a mile away is the 6-acre Painswick Rococo Garden around the Palladian mansion, Painswick House. The garden has been restored to the way it looked in an 18th century painting.

Painswicks Geschichte dreht sich um Schafe und Eiben. Der Wollehandel und die damit verwandte Branche für gefärbte Textilien brachte dem kleinen Marktstädtchen im 17. und 18. Jahrhundert angenehmen Wohlstand. Heute kommen die Besucher jedoch, um die gestutzten Eiben im Friedhof von St Mary zu sehen. Hier stehen angeblich 99 dieser Bäume, von denen die meisten gegen Ende des 18. Jahrhunderts gepflanzt wurden. Nach einer Legende wachsen jeweils nur 99, weil der Teufel den hundertsten Baum immer zerstört. Die Bäume werden jedes Jahr im September gestutzt, ein Vorgang, um den sich eine Zeremonie entwickelt hat.

L'histoire de Painswick est une histoire de brebis et d'ifs. En effet, le commerce de la laine (avec l'activité de teinture qui en découla) a rendu cette petite ville de marché prospère aux 17ème et 18ème siècles. Mais ce sont les ifs du cimetière de St Mary's qui attirent les touristes. Il comprend soi-disant 99 ifs taillés, la plupart plantés à la fin du 18ème siècle. Selon la légende, seuls 99 de ces arbres ne pousseront à la fois, car le diable a détruit le centième. Ces arbres sont taillés en septembre et une cérémonie est maintenant organisée à cette occasion.

SLAD

Immortalised by the poet and author Laurie Lee in his book Cider with Rosie, Slad is a small sleepy village strung along a minor road on a steep sided valley. Enthusiasts can identify the places Lee mentioned in his childhood reminiscences - including the Elizabethan Steanbridge squire's house and the Victorian church.

Slad ist ein kleines, verschlafenes Dorf, das sich an einer kleinen Straße in einem Tal mit steilen Hängen entlangzieht. Es wurde von dem Poeten und Schriftsteller Laurie Lee in seinem Buch "Cider with Rosie" verewigt.

Immortalisé par le poète et écrivain, Laurie Lee, dans son livre "Cider with Rosie", Slad est un petit village paisible qui s'étale le long d'une petite route dans une vallée aux flans escarpés.

STROUD

Stroud stands where five valleys meet. The abundant soft water, vital for the wool industry, ensured Stroud's position as the dominant Cotswold cloth centre since the 15th century. Its heyday was the late 18th, early 19th centuries when there were some 150 mills around the town. It became world famous for the dyed scarlet or blue military or naval cloth produced here. The wealth brought by the trade is reflected in Stroud's architectural heritage: the Subscription Rooms, built in 1833 where local functions are held; the market place called the Shambles, once the old meat market; the 16th century Town Hall.

Stroud liegt am Treffpunkt von fünf Tälern. Der reiche Vorrat an weichem Wasser, das für die Wolleindustrie unerläßlich war, garantierte dem Ort seit dem 15. Jahrhundert seine Stellung als das dominierende Textilzentrum der Cotswolds.

Der Reichtum, den der Handel Stroud einbrachte, spiegelt sich im architektonischen Erbe des Ortes wieder: Die "Subscription Rooms" aus dem Jahr 1833, in denen örtliche Veranstaltungen abgehalten wurden, der Marktplatz mit dem Namen "The Shambles", der früher der alte Fleischmarkt war, und die Stadthalle aus dem 16. Jahrhundert.

Stroud est le point de jonction de cinq vallées. L'eau douce abondante, vitale pour l'industrie de la laine, a donné à Stroud sa position de centre d'étoffes dominant des Cotswolds depuis le 15ème siècle.

La richesse apportée par ce secteur se reflète dans le patrimoine architectural de

Stroud; Les Subscription Rooms, construites en 1833 qui accueillent des réceptions; la place du marché qui s'appelle "The Shambles" et était autrefois le marché de la viande; la mairie du 16ème siècle.

SWAINSWICK

Legend tells the tale that Bladud, a king's son in the mists of time, firstly discovered the miraculous healing properties of Bath's mineral waters. He then took his herd of pigs, crossed the river Avon at Swineford and then finally settled in the village of Swainswick (or Swineswick).

The village is some three miles from Bath's centre. The man who was responsible for designing much of Bath's elegant architecture - John Wood - was buried in Swainswick churchyard in 1754.

Swainswick today looks much as it did then. Many of the village houses quaintly turn their backs to the world and present their fronts to the gardens and not the street.

St Mary's church features a noted Norman inner door. The manor house dates back to the 13th century.

Eine uralte Legende erzählt, daß Bladud, ein Königssohn, Dank seiner Schweine als erster die wundersamen Heilkräfte des Mineralwasser von Bath

entdeckte. Er überquerte dann bei Swineford mit seiner Schweineherde den Fluß Avon und ließ sich schließlich im Dorf Swainswick (auch Swineswick) nieder.

Das Dorf liegt knapp fünf Kilometer vom Stadtzentrum von Bath entfernt. John Wood, der einen Großteil der eleganten Architektur von Bath entwarf, wurde 1754 im Friedhof von Swainswick begraben.

D'après la légende, Bladud, un fils de roi dans la nuit des temps, découvrit tout d'abord les propriétés curatives miraculeuses des eaux minérales de Bath. Il traversa ensuite l'Avon avec son troupeau de cochons à Swineford, et finit par s'installer dans le village de Swainswick (ou Swineswick).

Le village est à cinq kilomètres du centre de Bath. L'homme qui a dessiné la plus grande partie de l'architecture élégante de Bath - John Wood - fut enterré dans le cimetière de Swainswick en 1754.

TETBURY

Tetbury's name derives from the Saxon abbess Tetta. The commercial centre of this small but picturesque market town is the 17th century Market House which is supported on 21 stout Tuscan pillars. Piercing the skyline is the Church of St Mary, built in 18th century Gothic style.

The Chipping is the old market place. From it, the ancient Chipping Steps lead to the area where the old monastery once stood.

The town features a Police Bygones Museum housed in old police cells. Gunstool Hill is the scene of the famous woolsack races on Spring Bank Holiday when contestants carry 65 lb woolsacks up and down the steep incline.

The mechanisation of the wool trade led to a recession in the town - which is why many of the 17th and 18th century houses remained largely unspoilt, to the delight of visitors today.

Just a mile away, at Doughton, is Highgrove House. This small, plain Cotswold mansion was built in the 18th century, badly damaged by fire at the end of the 19th century and became a centre of international interest in the 20th century after it was bought by the Prince of Wales in 1980 for £800,000. The town of Tetbury presented the Prince and Princess with a new set of entrance gates and the house interior has been renovated and the small estate transformed from a mixed farm to landscaped grassed parkland.

Between Tetbury and Stroud lies Gatcombe Park, the home of the Princess Royal.

Der Name der Stadt Tetbury geht auf die sächsische Äbtissin Tetta zurück. Das geschäftliche Zentrum dieses kleinen, aber malerischen Marktstädtchens ist das Market House aus dem 17. Jahrhundert mit seinen 21 dicken toskanischen Säulen. Die Silhouette der Stadt wird von der Kirche von St Mary unterbrochen, die im gothischen Stil des 18. Jahrhunderts erbaut ist.

In nur eineinhalb Kilometer Entfernung von Tetbury, bei Doughton, liegt Highgrove House. Dieses kleine, einfache Cotswolds-Herrenhaus aus dem 18. Jahrhundert wurde 1980 für 800.000 englische Pfund vom Prinzen von Wales gekauft. Die Stadt Tetbury schenkte dem Prinzen und der Prinzessin einen Satz neuer Einfahrtstore. Das Innere des Hauses wurde renoviert und das kleine Gut aus einem landwirtschaftlichen Betrieb zu Grünland mit Parkanlagen umgestaltet.

Le nom "Tetbury" provient de l'abbesse saxonne Tetta. Le centre commercial de cette petite ville de marché pittoresque est la Market House du 17 ème siècle supportée par 21 piliers toscans résistants. On peut voir la flèche de l'église St Mary, de style gothique du 18ème siècle, s'élancer majestueusement dans le ciel.

A un peu moins de 2 km, se trouve Highgrove House, à Doughton. Prince Charles a acheté, en 1980, ce petit manoir sobre des Cotswolds, construit au 18ème siècle, pour la somme de £ 800.000. La ville de Tetbury a offert au Prince et à la Princesse de Galles des nouvelles portes d'entrée; l'intérieur de la maison a été rénové et le petit domaine transformé - jadis une exploitation agricole mixte, il est devenu un parc paysager.